World War Two Br

Living History

Keith Goodman

Published by G-L-R (Great Little Read)

Written by Keith Goodman

This book has been created to entertain and educate young minds and is packed with information and trivia and lots of authentic images that bring the topic alive.

There is a fun quiz at the end to test how much has been learned.

TABLE OF CONTENTS

Introduction

The Second World War (WW2) was a conflict fought between the Allied Powers of Britain, France, the Soviet Union, and the USA and the Axis Powers of Germany, Italy, and Japan. Almost every country on the planet became involved, and over seventy million people lost their lives because of it.

World War Two was the deadliest in human history.

The war started in Europe but soon spread to the rest of the world. Most of the fighting took place in Europe, North Africa, and Southeast Asia.

This book tells the story of the main events

The Countdown to World War Two

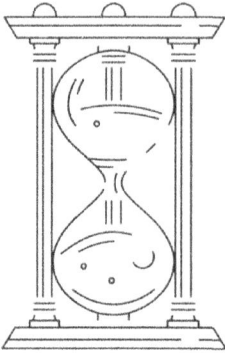

The date was **January 30, 1933**, and Adolph Hitler became the new German Chancellor. He was the popular leader of the Nazi Party and would become the dictator of the German people.

On **October 25, 1936,** Germany and Italy formed an alliance called the Rome-Berlin Axis Treaty.

On the **25th of November 1936**, Germany and Japan signed the Anti-Comintern Pact. This was an agreement against the Soviet Union.

In **July 1937**, Japanese troops invaded China.

On **March 12, 1938**, Hitler joined Austria with Germany in a pact called the Anschluss. Europe was now very close to war.

The New German Leader

Hitler was destined to become the leader of Germany

In the early 1930s, Adolph Hitler used the terrible economic conditions to gain power. Germany was frustrated with the food shortages, and poverty and Hitler blamed the harsh peace terms of the First World War. Hitler was a very charismatic speaker and offered the German people hope for the future.

Hitler and his Nazi Party became the most powerful in Germany, and President Paul von Hindenburg was forced to name him as Chancellor.

Hitler got rid any opposition and set Germany up as a one-party state with himself as the leader.

In 1936, Germany and Italy signed a treaty of friendship between the two countries and formed what became known as the Rome-German Axis. The leader of Italy was a dictator named Benito Mussolini. Later in the year, Germany and Japan signed an anti-communist agreement.

By 1940, Italy, Germany, and Japan had signed a Tripartite Pact to form the three Axis powers. The pact was intended to keep the USA from entering the war.

Germany took over Austria

Things began to heat up in Europe when German troops marched across the border on March 12, 1938, and entered Austria. The aim was to join all German-speaking people into what Hitler called the Third Reich (Third Empire).

Hitler set up a government that was favorable to the two nations joining together. The Anschluss (coming together) was confirmed, and from then on, Austria became a federal state ruled by Germany. This continued until the war ended and the independence of Austria was re-established.

Timeline 1939

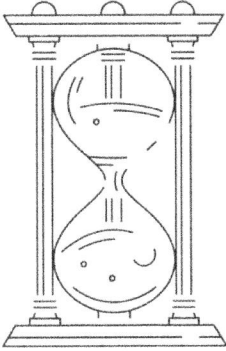

On **September 1, 1939**, Germany invaded Poland, and the Second World War started.

On **September 3, 1939**, Britain and France declared war on Germany

The German Invasion of Poland

In 1934, Hitler signed a nonaggression pact with Poland. Under the peace terms of the First World War, Poland had been given the German Provinces of Silesia, Poznan, and West Prussia. Many Germans wanted this land back.

During this period, Britain and France stood by and watched as Germany rearmed. This was against the Treaty of Versailles that was signed after the First World War. Looking back, it is clear that neither Britain nor France had the stomach for another war. The French and British Governments thought that by backing down to Germany, they could avoid another conflict.

Despite allowing Germany to take over the Sudetenland from Czechoslovakia, France and Britain were clear that they would not allow Germany to invade Poland. Hitler's usual excuse was that he wanted to join the German-speaking people of Europe into one nation. Three million Germans were living under Czechoslovakian rule. In Poland, Hitler claimed that Germans were being mistreated.

Although Hitler hated Stalin and the Soviet Union, the German-Soviet Pact was signed in August 1939. This pact secretly stated that Poland was to be divided between Germany and the Soviet Union (Russia).

Using the persecution of Germans as an excuse to attack, German troops and tanks crossed into Poland on September 1, 1939. A few days later, France and Britain declared war.

The Polish army could not stop the Germans and Russians, and the country was divided up with the River Bug as the border between German and Soviet troops.

Timeline 1940

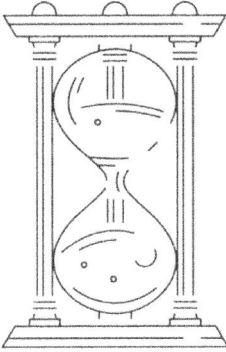

On the **9ᵗʰ of April**, Germany invaded Denmark and Norway. By June 9ᵗʰ, Germany was in control.

Between **May and June 1940**, German troops took control of Holland, Belgium, and Northern France.

Between **May 26 and June 4, 1940**, trapped British troops were miraculously evacuated by boats and ships from Dunkirk.

In Britain, Winston Churchill was made Prime Minister in **May 1940**.

In **June 1940**, Italy entered the war on the side of Germany.

In **July 1940**, Germany started to attack Britain by air. These attacks carried on until the end of October and became known as the Battle of Britain.

On **September 22, 1940**, Japan, Italy, and Germany signed the Axis Alliance, known as the Tripartite Pact.

The Dunkirk Evacuation

The rapid advance of the German Army backed up by the air force (Luftwaffe) took Britain and France by surprise. The invasion of Holland, Belgium, and France forced Allied troops to retreat. Holland and Belgium surrendered, and by the end of May, Allied troops were trapped on the beaches of a small French Port called Dunkirk.

The British leaders decided to bring the troops back to Britain. They collected every type of boat to transport the soldiers, but the process would be slow and extremely dangerous.

Even though the Germans had successfully reached the coast of France and defeated the Dutch, British, Belgian, and French armies, the evacuation of 340,000 troops was nothing more than a miracle. However, most of Britain's tanks, trucks, and heavy equipment were left in France.

Germany conquered the whole of France soon after the Dunkirk evacuation.

Around 850 private boats sailed out of the English port of Ramsgate to rescue the troops in Dunkirk. It was called Operation Dynamo. Contrary to the myth that members of the public sailed these civilian boats, the fact is that they were mostly sailed by members of the Royal Navy.

Trivia

Hitler ordered the German troops to stop advancing on Dunkirk. This allowed the trapped Allied troops to get away. Why did Hitler give this order? It is not clear, but probably he thought that the Luftwaffe attacking the beaches would be enough to stop the British and French from escaping.

The German planes dropped leaflets onto the beaches, calling for the soldiers to give up and surrender.

The Battle of Britain

Spitfires played a big part in defending Britain

One of the most important battles of World War Two (WW2) was the Battle of Britain.

When the British troops had been evacuated from Dunkirk, Germany had already conquered most of Europe, and Britain stood alone.

Hitler wanted to invade Britain but realized that to do so; he would first have to defeat the Royal Air Force (RAF). The battle of Britain occurred when German bombers crossed the English Channel from France and started to bomb Britain.

The name 'Battle of Britain' came from Winston Churchill's (Prime Minister of Britain) speech after France had been conquered. In his speech he said the Battle of France was over, and the Battle of Britain was about to start.

The Battle of Britain started on July 10, 1940, and lasted for many months.

The Germans were preparing to invade Britain and attacked coastal towns to destroy their defenses.

The RAF defended the coast and proved to be a very formidable opponent for the German Luftwaffe. Because of this, the Germans began to focus their efforts on destroying RAF airfields and radar stations.

Hitler became frustrated with the lack of success and switched his tactics to bombing London and other large cities.

September 15, 1940, was a day when the German Luftwaffe launched a massive attack on London. The RAF shot down many German planes, and it became clear that the British were far from defeated. After this date, the raids got less and less as Hitler realized he could not defeat the RAF, who were very well organized.

The German air force had more planes and pilots, but the British had radar, which could tell them in advance that German aircraft were crossing the English Channel.

Trivia

Hitler named the plan to invade Britain, Operation Sea Lion.

In the Battle of Britain, around 1,000 British planes were shot down, and 1,800 German planes.

The German air force used the Messerschmitt Bf109 and Bf110, the Heinkel HE111, Dornier DO17, Junker JU88 and the Junker JU 87.

The British air force used the Supermarine Spitfire, Hawker Hurricane, and the Boulton Paul Defiant.

The head of the Luftwaffe was Herman Goering. The chief of the RAF was Sir Hugh Dowding.

The German bombing of London was ferocious and lasted until 1941. This was called the Blitz, and at one stage of the war, London was bombed for 57 consecutive nights.

The bombing of London was finally stopped when Hitler needed his planes to invade the Soviet Union.

The Battle of the Atlantic

The Battle of the Atlantic was ongoing throughout WW2, as the British navy fought the German Navy for control of the sea.

The British needed to use the Atlantic as a supply line for food and weapons. The Germans wanted to stop the supply ships from getting through.

The Battle of the Atlantic was fought in the Northern Atlantic. When the USA entered the war, it spread to the coast of the USA and the Caribbean.

The battle lasted from 1939 until 1945.

In the beginning, the German U-Boats (submarines) sank many supply ships. Because of this, the German government ordered more

U-Boats to be constructed. By the middle of the war, there were hundreds on patrol in the Atlantic.

To counteract the U-boats, the British organized their ships into convoys with warships as escorts. The convoys were initially very successful, but as the Germans built more submarines, the convoy system (Lots of ships traveling together) became less successful.

The battle was at its most intense in 1943. A turning point was when the Allies broke the German codes and developed a new bomb called 'The Hedgehog' to sink the submarines.

As 1943 ended, it became clear that the Battle of the Atlantic had turned in favor of the Allies.

The control of the Atlantic was vital to Britain. The Germans never effectively stopped supplies from getting through, which meant that the British could keep fighting.

Both sides sustained heavy losses.

The Allies lost about 3,500 merchant ships and 175 warships. The German navy lost over 783 submarines.

Trivia

In 1941, Winston Churchill first called it the Battle of the Atlantic

At least 20 supply ships a day were needed to keep Britain in a position to carry on fighting.

The year 1942 was the worst for the Allies. They lost around 1,664 merchant ships.

Often, more than one submarine would attack a convoy. A group of submarines working together was called a Wolf Pack.

Allied plane crews used a giant light called the Leigh Light to spot surfaced U-boats at night.

Timeline 1941

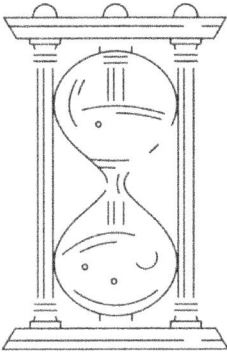

In **June 1941**, the Germans and Axis forces invaded the Soviet Union with over four million troops.

On **December 7, 1941**, the Japanese attacked US navy ships in Pearl Harbour. The next day, the USA came into the war on the side of the Allies.

The Invasion of the Soviet Union (Russia)

The codename for the invasion of Russia was Operation Barbarossa. It started on June 22, 1941, and involved over three million troops. The attack was across the Russian border, which stretched for 1,800 miles (2,900kilometres), and was the largest military invasion ever.

The Axis forces had more than 600,000 vehicles and 750,000 horses.

Hitler's main aim was to destroy the Russian military machine and capture the country's rich natural resources, including oil fields.

Unfortunately for Germany, the attack, which should have started in May, was delayed until June, and the Russian winter came early that year.

The German troops were not prepared for the severity of a Russian winter, and many of them only had summer clothes.

The Russian army was used to fighting in freezing conditions and was able to push the Axis forces back.

The Russians followed the German retreat all of the way to the gates of Berlin. The Battle of Berlin was the final battle of the war.

After this, the German Government surrendered.

The most famous conflict of the war in Russia was the Siege of Stalingrad.

The Battle of Stalingrad

The Battle of the city of Stalingrad was one of the biggest and deadliest of WW2.

This was the turning point of the war in the east, and Germany never recovered from the defeat.

The city was located on the Volga River in the southwest of Russia. Stalingrad was named after the Russian leader, Joseph Stalin, and was a major center for communications and industry.

The battle took place at the end of 1942 and the beginning of 1943. The Germans eventually surrendered to the Russians in February 1943, and Hitler was furious. He had wanted his troops to fight until death.

A massive mistake by the German High Command was to bomb the city. When the Germans eventually began the attack, the Russian troops hid in the rubble and the sewers under the city. The battle in the snow amongst the ruins was a fight that the Germans were not prepared for.

Eventually, the Russian troops started a counter-attack and trapped the Germans inside the city. In the end, lack of food and freezing conditions forced German General Paulus to surrender.

More than 750,000 Germans died in Stalingrad and around 500,000 Russians.

Trivia

Hitler was so angry with General Paulus for surrendering that he stripped him of his rank and called for a German national day of mourning for the shame.

Reducing the city to rubble meant that the German tanks could not operate properly.

About 91,000 German and Axis troops were captured at the end of the battle.

The Attack on Pearl Harbour

On Sunday, the 7th of December 1941, Japanese planes attacked the US Navy base at Pearl Harbor without warning. They attacked and destroyed many American warships and killed a lot of American soldiers and sailors. The USA declared war the next day.

Pearl Harbor is situated in Hawaii on the island of O'ahu. Hawaii at the time was US territory and not a state.

Even though the fighting in Europe was now in its second year, the USA had remained neutral. The Japanese had been overrunning parts of Asia and saw the American presence in Hawaii as a threat.

The Japanese commanders believed that if they sank enough American ships in Pearl harbor that the Americans would not have the stomach to fight back. The opposite happened, and the Americans declared war the next day.

The Japanese attack came as a complete shock to America, and hundreds of Japanese planes dropped bombs and torpedoes.

Two attack waves inflicted a lot of damage, but this damage was soon repaired, as the Japanese did not attack the repair facilities, ammunition sites, and oil tanks.

Most of the American ships were repaired, although the Arizona, the Utah, and the Oklahoma were beyond repair.

The USS Arizona was the biggest loss, with over 1,000 military personnel killed

Although America was in a state of shock after the attack, it had the effect of uniting the country into defeating the Japanese.

On the 8th of December, the USA declared war on Japan.

Three days later, Germany and Italy declared war on the USA.

Trivia

Apparently, the Japanese had meant to declare war on America before the attack on Pearl Harbor, but no message was ever received.

In the words of the American President, Roosevelt, December the 7th would be a date that would live in infamy.

The Japanese also used submarines in the attack.

The attack lasted 110 minutes.

The Japanese attacked on a Sunday because they thought that the Americans would be off guard.

Timeline 1942

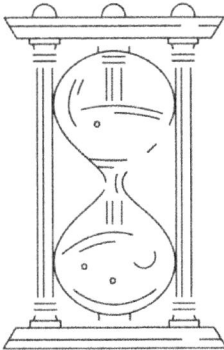

On June the 4th, 1942, the US Navy defeat the Japanese Navy at the Battle of Midway.

The Battle of Midway

Japanese Battleship Yamato was at the battle with its commander directing operations

One of the battles that turned out to be a turning point in WW2 was the Battle of Midway. It took place in the Pacific and started on the 4th of July. After four days of fierce fighting, the USA was victorious.

The island of Midway is situated right in the middle of the Pacific Ocean between the USA and Asia. It is 2,500 miles from Japan and 4,642 miles from the US coast.

In April 1942, America launched its first attack on Japanese soil. The Doolittle Raid was an air raid on Tokyo, which was the Japanese capital. The attack showed that the Japanese mainland was within striking distance of American bombers. Not only did it act as a morale boost to the US public, but it also was retaliation for Pearl Harbour.

The Japanese decided to attack the American base at Midway in an attempt to make the American forces retreat.

The attack by the Japanese was supposed to be secret, but the Americans had broken the codes and knew about it.

On the 4th of June 1942, the Japanese attacked with fighter planes and bombers. The planes were launched from four aircraft carriers.

The Americans had three aircraft carriers in the region. These were the Yorktown, the Enterprise, and the Hornet.

The Japanese attacked Midway, and the Americans attacked the Japanese aircraft carriers, and three of them were sunk.

The Yorktown attacked the remaining Japanese Battleship, the Hiryu. Both aircraft carriers were sunk in the conflict.

Losing four aircraft carriers was a terrific blow to the Japanese war machine. The Japanese also lost several other ships, 3,000 sailors, and 248 warplanes.

This was the first big victory for the Americans against the Japanese.

Trivia

Midway Island is now US territory.

The Japanese thought that there were only two American aircraft carriers in the region. They thought that the Yorktown was still being repaired.

Midway was used after the battle as a base for seaplanes and a submarine refueling port.

Timeline 1943

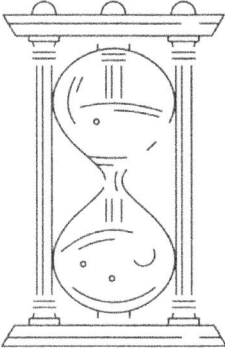

On **July 10, 1943**, the Allies invaded the Italian Island of Sicily.

On **September 3, 1943**, Italy surrendered to the Allies, and Germany helped the Italian leader, Mussolini, escape. He set up a government in the north of Italy.

The Italian Campaign

The Italian Campaign was the name given to the Allied attack on Italy in 1943.

The Allied forces swept through North Africa, and a British-American invasion of Sicily started in July 1943. The German troops could not prevent the island from being captured but escaped to the mainland to set up more defenses.

Even though the Italian Government surrendered in September 1943, the German forces continued fighting against the Allied advance. The advance was slow, but the Germans were gradually pushed back towards the north of the country.

With the fall of Rome and the beginning of the campaign in France, Italy became of secondary importance to the Allies.

The Italian Leader, Mussolini, set up a government in the North of Italy after being deposed by his own Grand Council, and then rescued by the Germans.

With the fall of the country imminent, he was caught trying to escape to Austria and executed by his own people.

Timeline 1944

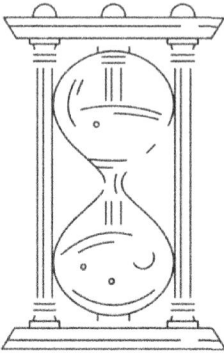

On **June the 6th, 1944**, Allied forces invaded France. Troops landed in Normandy and started to push the Germans back through France.

The Allies liberated Paris on **August 25, 1944**.

On **December 16, 1944**, the Germans launched a counter-attack in a last effort to win the war. This was called the Battle of the Bulge.

The Normandy Landings

After suffering the humiliation of Dunkirk at the hands of the Germans, the British, along with their allies, returned to France on June 6, 1944. The Allied force consisted of British, American, French, and Canadian troops. Around 150,000 soldiers landed on the beaches of Normandy in France in a campaign that was called D-Day. The Normandy landings were the turning point in WW2.

Germany had succeeded in taking control of Northern Europe but failed to invade Britain. The D-Day landings started with airstrikes, which destroyed key airfields, railroads, and bridges. The Germans were aware that an invasion was coming, but they didn't know where. The Allies tried their best to confuse the Germans into thinking that the attack was coming in the north of Normandy. The Germans also thought an attack on the French port of Calais was a possibility.

The invasion planning took a lot of time, but the weather almost meant that it was called off. Eventually, it was agreed to continue with the planned date, and the first wave started with paratroopers.

Paratroopers jumped out of planes with parachutes. They jumped at night and landed behind the German troops. These paratroopers had the task of destroying key targets and capturing bridges.

As well as paratroopers, the RAF dropped bombs on the German defenses. The French Resistance (local population) cut communication wires and blew up railway lines.

The main invasion force consisted of over 6,000 ships that carried the troops and equipment.

American troops landed on the Utah and Omaha beaches. The Utah landing was a success, but there was a lot of German resistance on the Omaha beach, and many of the invaders died. However, they eventually succeeded in taking the beach.

By the time D-Day had finished, more than 150,000 Allied troops had landed in Normandy. As these troops gradually moved inland, more troops arrived. The Germans slowly retreated.

By the 17th of June, there were more than 500,000 Allied troops in France.

Trivia

The attack needed to take place during a full moon. Because of this, there were just a couple of days that were possible during the month. The overall name of the invasion was called Operation Overlord, but the landings were called Operation Neptune.

The German High Command thought that Normandy was the least likely place for the attack as it was a long way from England and there was no port.

The battle of the Bulge

This was the last attempt by Germany to push back the Allied advance. However, for Germans dreaming of another Dunkirk, there would be disappointment.

There was a feeling by many military experts that after the Normandy landings the war was drawing to an end. Hitler had other ideas, and in December 1944, the Germans advanced through the Ardennes Forest and went on the offensive.

The German attack was massive and involved 1,000 tanks and 200,000 troops. The plan was to break through the American defences. The plan had an element of surprise and initially worked.

The German troops were victorious and broke through the American defenses. The Battle of the Bulge is best remembered for the many instances where small units of American soldiers attacked or held out against the advancing Germans.

The American troops held the line until reinforcements arrived, and from then on, the Germans were held and eventually pushed back or captured.

The Germans advance caused a 'bulge' in the American defenses. They advanced for about 60 miles. The fierce American resistance and the lack of supplies eventually turned defeat into victory for the Allies.

The Germans had 100,000 casualties and dead and the Americans 80,000.

Much of the German strength was lost after the battle, and from then on, it was only a matter of time before WW2 would be over.

Trivia

The German tanks ground to a halt because they ran out of fuel during the battle. A lot of German fuel depots had been destroyed by American bombing.

The 3rd Army under General Patton was able to come to the rescue after a couple of days.

The battle started on December 16, 1944, and ended on January 25, 1945.

Timeline 1945

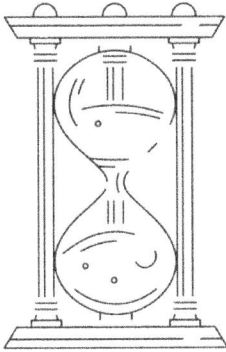

US Marines captured the island of Iwo Jima on **February 19, 1945**.

On **April 12, 1945,** the President of the USA, Franklin Roosevelt, died and is replaced by Harry Truman.

US troops crossed the German River Rhine on **March 22, 1945**.

On **April 30, 1945**, Adolph Hitler killed himself because he knew that Germany had lost the war.

Germany surrendered on **May 7, 1945**.

The USA dropped an atomic bomb on the Japanese city of Hiroshima on **August 6, 1945**. Even though the city was destroyed, the Japanese didn't surrender.

On **August 9, 1945,** the USA dropped an atomic bomb on the Japanese city of Nagasaki.

On **September 2, 1945**, Japan surrendered, and World War Two was over.

The Battle of Berlin

The last European battle of WW2 was the Battle of Berlin. It started on April 16, 1945, and ended on May 2.

The battle was fought between the German Army and the Soviet Army.

The Soviet Army consisted of around 2,500,000 troops, 7,500 planes, and 6,500 tanks.

The German forces consisted of 1,000,000 soldiers, 2,200 planes, and 1,500 tanks.

Because the fighting had depleted the German Army, many young boys and old men were recruited to defend the city.

The Russian troops attacked the outskirts of the city and defeated the German defenders.

This allowed them to move into the city itself.

The city was bombed and surrounded.

Hitler realized that there was no hope left of a peace deal and committed suicide.

The fighting was fierce in the city, but the end was inevitable.

The Germans surrendered unconditionally to the Soviet Army, and the war in Europe was over.

Trivia

The city of Berlin was reduced to rubble, and thousands of civilians were killed.

As well as Soviet troops, there were 150,000 Polish soldiers.

After the battle, there were around one million Germans who were homeless.

The Atomic Bomb

In the late 1930s, scientists theorized that by splitting the atom, they could produce a powerful explosion that was much stronger than any bomb that had previously been invented. During the war, both sides raced to see who could develop the atom bomb first.

Albert Einstein had many theories that helped in the creation of the atomic bomb. When the world realized that it was just a matter of time before someone made one, there was a fear about what would happen if Hitler could make the first bomb.

The Manhattan Project was set up in America to develop the world's first atomic bomb.

The first atomic weapon was exploded in July 1945 in the New Mexico desert.

Germany surrendered before the first atomic bomb was made. Japan, however, had still not surrendered.

Rather than an American invasion, which would cost lives, it was decided to use the atomic bomb to force Japan to surrender.

The first bomb (called Little Boy) was dropped on Hiroshima in Japan on August 6, 1945. Thousands of people were killed.

Despite the terrible loss of life, the Japanese refused to surrender, so another bomb was dropped on Nagasaki on August 9, 1945 (this bomb was called Fat Man).

The Japanese finally surrendered on September 2, 1945.

Trivia

The first bomb was built with uranium, but the second bomb used the more powerful plutonium.

An estimated 135,000 people died in Hiroshima and 70,000 in Nagasaki.

World War Two Quiz

1 What year did Germany invade Poland?

2 What was the name of the Prime Minister of Britain in May 1940?

3 From which port in France were Allied troops evacuated back to Britain in 1940?

4 Which country did Germany invade in June 1941?

5 What was the name of the American aircraft carrier that was sunk at the Battle of Midway?

6 What happened on June 6, 1944?

7 What was the name of the battle that started with a German advance through the Ardennes Forest?

8 What was Fat Man?

Thank you for Reading this Book

Other Books in the Living History Series

1 Ancient Britain for Kids

2 Roman Britain for kids

3 Anglo-Saxon Britain for Kids

4 Viking Britain for Kids

5 Norman Britain for Kids

6 Plantagenet England for Kids

7 Tudor England for Kids

8 17th Century England for Kids

9 Georgian Britain for Kids

10 Victorian Britain for Kids

11 Britain at War for Kids

12 World War Two Britain for Kids

You can visit the English Reading Tree Page by clicking:

Visit Amazon's Keith Goodman Page (Mailing List)

Books in the History Detective Series

1 The Boston Tea Party

2 Sink The Lusitania

Books in the English Reading Tree Series by Keith Goodman include:

1 The Titanic for Kids

2 Shark Facts for Kids

3 Solar System Facts for Kids

4 Dinosaur Facts for Kids

5 American Facts and Trivia for Kids

6 Christmas Facts and Trivia for Kids

7 Space Race Facts for Kids

8 My Titanic Adventure for Kids

9 Save the Titanic for Kids

38 The History of Ancient Weapons

39 Titanic Conspiracy Theories for Kids

40 The Ancient Romans for Kids

41 Famous Americans for Kids

42 Twentieth Century Heroes and Villains for Kids

43 The Ancient Aztecs for kids

44 Wild West History for Kids

45 All about Birds for Kids

46 All about Reptiles for Kids

47 The Renaissance Explained for Kids

48 The French Revolution Explained for Kids

49 Important Battles of World War Two

50 Key events that created America

51 Ancient China

66 1917 for Kids

67 The Titanic Diary for Kids

68 Myths and Legends for Kids

69 The Loch Ness Monster for Kids

70 Ghost Stories for Kids

71 More UFO Stories for Kids

72 More Ghost Stories for Kids

Other books by the same author:

Meet the Boneheads

The School Bully: Meet the Boneheads

Books From the For School Series

1 Native American History for School Grades 3 – 5

2 Colonial American History for School Grades 3 – 5

3 The American Revolution for School Grades 3 – 5

4 The American Industrial Revolution for School Grades 3 – 5

5 The American Civil War for School Grades 3 – 5

Quiz Answers

1 1939

2 Winston Churchill

3 Dunkirk

4 The Soviet Union (Russia)

5 The Yorktown

6 D-Day or the Normandy landings.

7 The battle of the Bulge

8 The name of the atomic bomb dropped on Nagasaki

Attributions

Soldier Author kuco Standard licence https://depositphotos.com/ ID 25944577

Egg-timer Author oleg_katya_yd Standard licence https://depositphotos.com/ ID 109289092

Hitler Author Wirestock Standard licence https://depositphotos.com/ ID 496432184

Egg-timer Author oleg_katya_yd Standard licence https://depositphotos.com/ ID 109289092

Invasion of Poland Author kuco Standard licence https://depositphotos.com/ ID 51143671

Egg-timer Author oleg_katya_yd Standard licence https://depositphotos.com/ ID 109289092

Dunkirk Author Furian Standard licence https://depositphotos.com/ ID 608988132

Spitfire Author tompic Standard licence https://depositphotos.com/ ID 71973581

Battleship Author Paylessimages Standard licence https://depositphotos.com/ ID 683099748

Egg-timer Author oleg_katya_yd Standard licence https://depositphotos.com/ ID 109289092

Invading Russia Author kuco Standard licence https://depositphotos.com/ ID 51127627

Stalingrad Author kuco Standard licence https://depositphotos.com/ ID 51143677

Japanese planes and flag Author 1981srb Standard licence
https://depositphotos.com/ ID 359565810

Egg-timer Author oleg_katya_yd Standard licence
https://depositphotos.com/ ID 109289092

Battleship Yamato Author deepdrilling Standard licence
https://depositphotos.com/ ID 712127594

Egg-timer Author oleg_katya_yd Standard licence
https://depositphotos.com/ ID 109289092

Italian campaign Author kuco Standard licence
https://depositphotos.com/ ID 51127749

Egg-timer Author oleg_katya_yd Standard licence
https://depositphotos.com/ ID 109289092

D-Day Author Tawng Standard licence https://depositphotos.com/
ID 28394935

Battle of Bulge Author mariamoskvitsova Standard licence
https://depositphotos.com/ ID 142052894

Egg-timer Author oleg_katya_yd Standard licence
https://depositphotos.com/ ID 109289092

Burning city Author Marsea Standard licence
https://depositphotos.com/ ID 303787538

Atomic bomb Author rfphoto Standard licence
https://depositphotos.com/ ID 195038916

Printed in Great Britain
by Amazon